FOOTSTEPS IN TIME

THE Greeks

Sally Hewitt

Contents

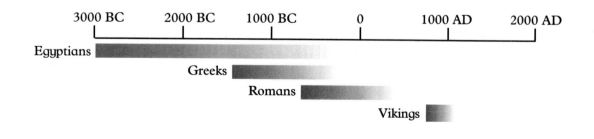

3000 BC   2000 BC   1000 BC   0   1000 AD   2000 AD

Egyptians

Greeks

Romans

Vikings

CP CHILDRENS PRESS ®

Who were the Greeks?

Greece is a land of mountains, valleys, and hundreds of islands. Ancient Greek cities were cut off from each other by the mountains. They traded with each other by sea. There were no kings in ancient Greece. Cities ruled themselves. Some, like Athens and Sparta, became very rich and powerful.

Greece

Aegean Sea

Athens

Mediterranean Sea

Crete

The people were divided into two groups – free people and slaves. Slaves were owned by free people. The slaves worked as servants and laborers. Citizens were wealthy free men. They took part in government and served in the army. Women looked after their houses and families.

The ancient Greeks loved art and learning. They built magnificent temples and theaters. Many great thinkers, mathematicians, and writers were Greek.

Greek writing

Only boys went to school. They wrote by scratching letters on a wooden tablet covered in melted wax.

You will need:

Thick cardboard   Thin cardboard   Pencil
Crayons   Brown paint   White glue

Follow the steps . . .

1. Paint the thick cardboard brown to look like a wooden tablet.

2. Color the thin cardboard with a colored crayon. Then cover the colored crayon with black crayon. Glue the cardboard onto the tablet.

3. Use the pencil to scratch your name in Greek letters. There were no letters for C, F, H, J, Q, V, W, X, Y. Make up your own letters for these.

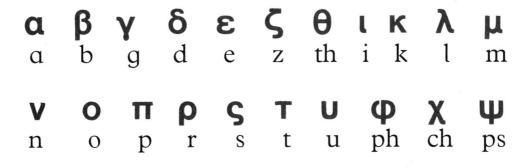

α	β	γ	δ	ε	ζ	θ	ι	κ	λ	μ
a	b	g	d	e	z	th	i	k	l	m

ν	ο	π	ρ	ς	τ	υ	φ	χ	ψ
n	o	p	r	s	t	u	ph	ch	ps

Knucklebones

Girls stayed home and learned how to run the house.
They played a game called knucklebones.

You will need:

Newspaper	Bowl	Water
White glue	Paint	

Follow the steps . . .

1. Put small pieces of newspaper into the bowl. Mix equal amounts of glue and water. Pour the mixture over the pieces to make papier-mâché.

2. Squeeze the papier-mâché into little knucklebone shapes. Let them dry. Paint them.

3. Throw the knucklebones into the air and try to catch them on the back of your hand.

Homes

The houses of wealthy city people were made of sun-dried mud bricks. The floors were made of beaten earth. Children played in a central courtyard that had an altar for family prayers and a well to supply water. Windows in the house were small and high to keep out the heat, the noise, the dirt, and the smell of the streets.

Men and women lived in separate parts of the house. The men held parties. They lay on couches while slaves served them food and drink.

Olive oil was used for washing. People rubbed it into their skin, scraped it off, and splashed themselves with cold water from a large basin.

Vase decoration

Black-figure and red-figure vases were popular.
They were often decorated with stories of the gods.

You will need:

Black paper	Orange paper	Pencil
Scissors	Glue	

Follow the steps . . .

1. Copy this vase shape.
   Cut out one black vase and two
   orange vases, exactly the same.

2. Draw a shape on the black vase
   and cut it out. Glue the shape
   onto one of the orange vases.
   This is a black-figure vase.

3. Glue the rest of the black vase
   onto the other orange vase
   to make a red-figure vase.

Clay figures

We have learned about the everyday life of the ancient Greeks from the little clay figures they made.

You will need:

Modeling clay   Modeling tool   Water

Follow the steps . . .

1. Make a small ball of clay for the head, a fat roll for the body, and long thin rolls for legs and arms.

2. Dampen the parts you want to stick. Then put the pieces together to make a figure.

3. Bend the arms and legs. Make the hair and face with the modeling tool. Leave the figure to dry.

4. Now make a model of yourself. Maybe someone will find it in 2,500 years!

A day at the theater

During the five-day festival of Dionysus in Athens, huge crowds filled the theater. People brought food and watched plays all day. Those who were too poor to pay were given free tickets.

Tragedies were serious plays that told stories of the gods and great heroes. Comedies were very funny, with jokes about politicians and well-known people.

Sport and games

Sport was very important in ancient Greece. It kept the young men fit and ready for war. The Olympic Games, held in honor of Zeus, were the biggest and most important games. Events included wrestling, chariot races, running, and javelin throwing. Winners received an olive wreath, a palm branch, and ribbons.

15

An Olympic torch

In the ancient Olympic Games, relay runners passed a torch to each other rather than a baton. The winner lit a fire to the gods.

You will need:

Black construction paper   Adhesive tape   Newspaper
White, orange, yellow, and red tissue paper

Follow the steps . . .

1. Cut out a half-circle of black paper and roll it into a cone shape. Tape the edges together.

2. Crumple some newspaper into a ball. Cut the white tissue paper into strips. Cut the colored tissue paper into flame shapes.

3. Push the ball of newspaper into the cone and tape the ends of the tissue paper onto it.

Theater masks

In ancient Greece, all actors were men. They wore masks with big, open mouths that made their voices louder.

You will need:

Cardboard	Newspaper	Scissors
String	Hole punch	Yarn
White glue	Paints and brush	

Follow the steps . . .

1. Copy the outline of the mask onto the cardboard. Cut it out. Punch holes in the tabs.

2. Dip small pieces of newspaper in a mixture of glue and water. Glue them all over the mask, especially near the eyebrows and mouth. Let the mask dry.

3. Paint the mask. Glue on strands of yarn for hair. Thread string through the tab holes.

19

Gods and legends

The Greeks believed that gods and goddesses watched over every part of their lives. The gods had to be pleased and obeyed. The Greeks made offerings to the gods outside the beautiful temples they built for them.

Zeus

Aphrodite

Hermes

Pluto

Athena

Hera

The most powerful gods were the twelve
Olympians, who lived on cloud-covered Mount
Olympus. The father of the gods was called
Zeus. When he threw his spear, thunder crashed
and lightning flashed across the sky.

Artemis

Apollo

Ares

Dionysus

Demeter

Poseidon

Medusa head

Greek legend said that people turned into stone if they looked at snake-haired Medusa the Gorgon.

You will need:

Construction paper   Cardboard   Pencil   Crayons
Green tissue paper   Scissors   Glue

Follow the steps . . .

1. Draw 16 snakes on the construction paper. Cut them out. Glue eyes and tongues on the snakes.

2. Curl the snakes by pulling a pair of closed scissors along the bodies.

3. Crumple a circle of tissue paper for Medusa's face. Glue it onto a cardboard circle. Add eyes, a nose, and a mouth.

4. Glue the snakes' tails around the edge of Medusa's head.

INDEX

Entries in *italics* are activity pages.

1995 Childrens Press Edition
© 1995 Watts Books, London, New York, Sydney
All rights reserved. Printed in USA
Published simultaneously in Canada.
    4 5 R 99

Editor: Annabel Martin
Consultant: Richard Tames
Design: Mike Davis
Artwork: Cilla Eurich and Ruth Levy
Photographs: Peter Millard

Library of Congress Cataloging-in-Publication Data:

Hewitt, Sally.
    The Greeks / by Sally Hewitt ; illustrated by
Cilla Eurich and Ruth Levy.
        p. cm. – (Footsteps in Time)
    ISBN 0-516-08057-1 (lib. bdg.) ISBN 0-516-26231-9 (pbk.)
    1. Greece–Civilization–To 146 B.C.–Juvenile
literature. [1. Greece–Civilization–To 146 B.C.]
I. Eurich, Cilla. ill. II. Levy, Ruth, ill. III. Title.
IV. Series: Footsteps in Time (Chicago, Ill.)
DF77.H58 1995   94-42232
938–dc20   CIP
                                      AC